THE AUSTRO-PRUSSIAN WAR
IN BOHEMIA, 1866

THE
AUSTRO-PRUSSIAN WAR
IN BOHEMIA, 1866

OTHERWISE KNOWN AS
THE SEVEN WEEKS' WAR
OR
NEEDLE-GUN WAR

BY

J. H. ANDERSON, F.R.Hist.Soc.

BARRISTER-AT-LAW; LATE LECTURER AT KING'S COLL., LONDON; SUCCESSFUL CANDIDATE
IN INDIAN CIVIL, AND HOME CIVIL (CLASS I.) EXAMINATIONS; LECTURER ON
MILITARY HISTORY AND STRATEGY AT 5, LEXHAM GARDENS, W.,
AND AT THE ROYAL UNITED SERVICE INSTITUTION

The Naval & Military Press Ltd

Published by

The Naval & Military Press Ltd
Unit 5 Riverside, Brambleside
Bellbrook Industrial Estate
Uckfield, East Sussex
TN22 1QQ England

Tel: +44 (0)1825 749494

www.naval-military-press.com
www.nmarchive.com

PREFACE

THIS campaign is prescribed for the Staff College Examination of 1908 and for the Promotion Examinations of May, 1908, and November, 1908. In the latter examinations special attention is to be given to the period June 26—July 3, and in both examinations officers need not go beyond July 4. The authorities on the campaign are numerous—the Prussian and Austrian official accounts, Glünicke's and Bonnal's excellent works, to the plans in which I would draw special attention. There are besides a United States account by A. L. Wagner, Hozier's well-known book, G. Addison's small work on the strategy, and Adams' " Great Campaigns in Europe," as well as the German account by H. Blankenburg, and Moltke's " Projects for 1866 " with its excellent map.

One of my difficulties has been to settle the spelling of the names, which constantly varies, and I append here a list of names that appear puzzling; the endings —c and —tz in Bohemian names are identical—e.g. Horitz = Horic.

Prelauc = Prelouc = Prschelautsch ;
Gitschin = Jicin ;
Prischowitz in the plan of Münchengrätz ;

Prossnitz in Moravia;

Parschnitz = Pranochnitz in the plan of Trautenau;

Deutsch Praussnitz near Kaile in the same plan;

Prauschnitz = Ober Praussnitz = Praussnitz, W. of Elbe R. and N. of Miletin;

Sichrow, S. of Liebenau;

Sichrow, near Münchengrätz, and S. of Iser R.;

Podol, where railway crosses Iser R.;

Podoll, S. of Sichrow near Münchengrätz;

Zittau = Littau, in Moravia;

Zittau in Saxony;

Zwittau in Moravia;

Reichenbach in Silesia;

Reichenberg in Bohemia;

Friedland in Moravia;

Friedland in Silesia; and in Bohemia;

Cerekwitz near Hohenmauth;

Cerekwitz near Königgrätz;

Kostelec near Eipel;

Kostelec S.E. of Königgrätz;

Libau = Liebau in Silesia;

Liebenau in Bohemia;

Nachod is on the R. Mettau;

Trautenau, Parschnitz, Eipel, Skalitz are on the R. Aupa, which in Glünicke's Map V. is incorrectly called the Mettau R.

LIST OF DATES

1866.	May 12.	Prussian Mobilisation ordered.
	May 30.	Moltke's orders, executed June 10.
	May 31.	Italy, Germany, and Austria on war-footing.
	June 2.	Prussian Mobilisation completed.
	June 10.	Benedek in Moravia; 1st Corps in Bohemia.
	June 11.	Moltke had full information *re* Austrians.
	June 12.	Moltke's orders, executed June 18.
	June 14.	Vote of the Diet.
	June 15.	War between Prussia and Hanover, Saxony, Hesse-Kassel.
	June 16.	Prussia invaded Hanover, Hesse-Kassel, and Saxony.
	June 17.	Saxons entered Bohemia.

1866. June 20. War between Prussia, Italy and
                 Allies, and Austria, Bavaria
                 and Allies.

       June 22. Moltke's Gitschin order.

       June 23. Frederick Charles invaded Bo-
                 hemia.

       June 24. Battle of Custozza.

       June 26. Action at Hühnerwasser; skir-
                 mish at Liebenau; action of
                 Podol (VIII. Division v. 1st
                 Corps); Austrian Cavalry
                 reported Crown Prince's
                 march.

       June 27. VI. Corps at Habelschwerdt;
                 action of Trautenau (I. Corps
                 v. 10th Corps); action of
                 Nachod (V. Corps v. 6th
                 Corps and 1st Reserve
                 Cavalry Division); combat
                 of Oswiecim.

       June 28. Action of Münchengrätz (Elbe
                 Army and V. Division v.
                 Saxon Prince's rearguard);
                 action of Soor or Burkers-
                 dorf (Guards v. 10th Corps);

1866.   action of Skalitz (V. Corps,
one Brigade of VI. Corps
and Guard Cuirassiers *v.* 8th
Corps); Benedek gave up his
third plan.

June 29.   Hanoverian Army surrendered
and Hesse-Kassel occupied ;
battle of Gitschin (V. Division
and III. Division *v.* Saxons
and 1st Corps) ; capture of
Königinhof (Guards *v.* 10th
Corps); action of Schweinschädel (V. Corps, VI. Corps,
and Guard Cuirassiers *v.* 4th
Corps).

June 30.   I. and II. Armies connected at
Arnau.

July 1.   1 a.m. Benedek retreated behind
the Bistritz.

July 2.   Telegraphic   communication
failed with the II. Army ;
Benedek decided on battle.

July 3.   Battle of Königgrätz.

CLOCK OF THE BATTLE

1866, July 3. 5 a.m. II. Army started.

6 a.m. Frederick Charles moved.

8 a.m. Guns opened ; Elbe Army occupied Nechanitz.

8.30 a.m. VII. Division on Benatek ;
VIII. Division crossed.

10 a.m. 3rd Corps at Lipa-Chlum ;
10th Corps at Langenhof.

11 a.m. to 3 p.m. Awful Austrian
gun-fire.

11 a.m. XV. Division crossed.

11.15 a.m. Crown Prince at Chote-
bovek.

11.30 a.m. Benedek learnt Crown
Prince's approach.

12 noon. VII. Division retired to
Benatek ; Saxon Prince
counter-attacked.

1 p.m. Danger of Frederick Charles;
I. Division Guards took
Horenowes.

1.30 p.m. V. Corps at Horenowes.

2.30 p.m. VI. Corps took Sendracic.

1866. July 3.   2.45 p.m. I. Division Guards
                 took Chlum.
       4.30 p.m. Austrians retreated.
       July 4.   Benedek on Olmütz, 10th Corps
                 and most of cavalry on
                 Vienna.
       July 6.   Prussians discovered Austrian
                 retreat.
       July 11. Benedek at Olmütz, Archduke
                 Albert in command.
       July 12-13. I. Army in Brünn. Elbe
                 Army in Znaim.
       July 15. Action of Tobitschau (I. Corps
                 and Cavalry Division Hart-
                 mann v. 8th and 1st
                 Corps).
       July 22. Combat of Blumenau (VII. and
                 VIII. Divisions and Cavalry
                 Division Hann v. Mondel);
                 armistice of Nikolsburg.
       August   Treaty of Prague.

PLANS OF BENEDEK

1. Offensive.
2. Mass near Josephstadt in a defensive position.

3. Move main body against I. Army, June 21, discarded June 28.
4. Fight at Dubenetz, June 28-30.
5. Retreat June 30—July 2.
6. Fight at Königgrätz, July 3.

CONTENTS

CHAPTER I

CHAPTER II

CHAPTER III

CHAPTER IV

CHAPTER V

CHAPTER VI

CHAPTER VII

14   CONTENTS

CHAPTER VIII

CHAPTER IX

CHAPTER X

CHAPTER XI

MAPS AND PLANS

The Austro-Prussian War in Bohemia, 1866.

CHAPTER I

CAUSES OF THE WAR

VARIOUS disputes had arisen between Austria Map IV. in Glü- and Prussia, whilst Bismarck made an alliance nicke. with Italy, who coveted the Austrian province of Map No. I. Venetia. He also bought off Napoléon III. by verbal promises of territorial aggrandisement on the N.E. of France. On June 14 the Federal Diet at Frankfurt, on the motion of Austria, voted the mobilisation of all the Confederation troops except the Prussian, whilst Prussia demanded that Saxony, Hanover, and Hesse-Kassel should reject the Diet's decision. Those states refused, and Prussian forces at once invaded them (June 16).

Prussia had for allies Italy (200,000 men), Saxe-Coburg-Gotha, Lippe, Oldenburg, Hanse Towns, all of whom totalled 28,000; Austria had for allies Bavaria (52,000), Saxony (24,000), Hanover (18,000), the Electorate of Hesse-Kassel (7,000), Würtemberg (16,000), Baden (10,000), the Grand Duchy of Hesse-Darmstadt (9,000), the Duchy of Hesse-Nassau (5,000). Total, 141,000.

CHAPTER II

MILITARY SYSTEMS

PRUSSIAN : they had had no experience of war, but they were a nation in arms, every man from 17 to 45 being liable to serve 2 years with the colours and then in various reserves. The Army was territorial, except the Guards, and included 8 corps and the Guard. Each corps equalled 2 infantry divisions and corps troops ; each division equalled 2 brigades; each brigade equalled 2 regiments ; each regiment equalled 3 battalions ; each battalion equalled 4 companies ; each company equalled 250 men. In each division were 1 cavalry regiment and 4 field batteries of 6 guns each. A Prussian division equalled 12,000 infantry, 480 cavalry, and 24 guns. Corps troops equalled 3 batteries of horse artillery and 4 batteries of field artillery (thus in an army corps there were 90 guns), 1 jäger battalion, 1 battalion of engineers, 1 battalion of A.S.C., and a cavalry brigade of 3 regiments. Besides these were 9 ammunition columns, 1 pontoon column, and 3 field hospitals. A Prussian army corps equalled 25,000 infantry, 2,400 cavalry, and 90 guns, except the Guard, which was about 6,000 stronger. The cavalry division included 16 squadrons, and numbered 1,920 horsemen and 12 guns, the squadrons being of 120 men. The total number of the Army and the Landwehr stood at 720,000; the Landsturm included all those not in the two former. All except the Landsturm were mobilised at the time of Königgrätz.

Austrian: the system allowed of exemptions being purchased. The term of service was 3 years with the colours and 7 years in the reserve. A great weakness was the disloyalty of the various races in the Empire, and mobilisation was much obstructed by the necessity of quartering Italian troops in Hungary and Hungarians in Venice. The cavalry and artillery were good, but the language question and want of initiative were evils. The railways were by no means good.

The Austrian numbers stood at 600,000, and the field army counted 10 army corps, of which 7 formed the Northern Army, with 5 cavalry divisions. An army corps equalled 4 brigades of infantry and corps troops; a brigade of infantry equalled 2 regiments and 1 jäger battalion, with a battery of 8 guns; a regiment equalled 3 battalions; a battalion equalled 6 companies; a company equalled 160 men. Corps troops equalled 1 cavalry regiment, 6 reserve batteries, 1 company engineers, 1 field ambulance.

CHAPTER III

THE ARMIES

SAXON army corps included two infantry divisions, a cavalry division and reserve artillery. Total, 20 battalions, 16 squadrons, 58 guns, and 2 engineer companies. Its commander was the Crown Prince of Saxony and its numbers 24,000.

Austrian Northern Army : General Benedek.

Chief of Staff, Henikstein ; Chief of Operations, Krizmanic.

1st Army Corps, under Clam Gallas, in five brigades :

    35 battalions, 5 squadrons, 88 guns.

        Total (+ 1st Light Cavalry Division) 36,000

2nd Army Corps, under Count Thun, in four brigades :

    28 battalions, 5 squadrons, 72 guns.

               Total .   . 31,000

3rd Army Corps in four brigades :

    28 battalions, 5 squadrons, 80 guns.

               Total .   . 23,000

4th Army Corps, under Festetic, in four brigades :

    28 battalions, 5 squadrons, 72 guns.

              Total .   . 31,000

6th Army Corps, under Ramming, in four brigades :

    28 battalions, 5 squadrons, 72 guns.

              Total .   . 30,000

8th Army Corps, under Archduke Leopold, in four brigades :

    27 battalions, 5 squadrons, 72 guns.

              Total .   . 31,000

10th Army Corps, under Gablenz, in four brigades :

    28 battalions and 72 guns.

              Total .   . 30,000

1st Light Cavalry Division, under Edelsheim :

    30 squadrons and 24 guns.

2nd Light Cavalry Division, under Prince Thurn and Taxis :

    20 squadrons and 16 guns.

              Total .   . 3,000

1st Reserve Cavalry Division :

    26 squadrons and 16 guns.

              Total .   . 4,000

2nd Reserve Cavalry Division:
26 squadrons and 16 guns.

Total . . 4,000

3rd Reserve Cavalry Division:
26 squadrons and 16 guns.

Total . . 4,000

Army Reserve Artillery:
128 guns.

Total: 202 battalions, 158 squadrons,
744 guns, and 7 engineer companies.

Total numbers . . 247,000

An Austrian army corps included 30,000 infantry, 600 cavalry, and 80 guns; an Austrian cavalry division included 3,000 horsemen and 12 guns, each squadron being of 120 men.

Prussian Armies: under King William; Chief of Staff, Moltke.

I. Army, under Prince Frederick Charles (the "Red Prince"), included:

			Batts.	Squads.	Guns
III. Infantry Division, Werder		}	25	16	78
IV. ,, ,, Herwarth					
V. ,, ,, Tümpling .			12	4	24
VI. ,, ,, Manstein .			13	5	24
VII. ,, ,, Fransecky .			12	4	24
VIII. ,, ,, Horn . .			10	4	24

Cavalry Corps under Prince Albert:
I. Cavalry Division, under Alvensleben,
21 squadrons.

II. Cavalry Division, under Hann, 20
squadrons.

Horse Artillery, 30 guns.

Army Reserve Artillery, 96 guns.

Total: 72 battalions, 74 squadrons, 300
guns (180 being rifled), and 3 engineer
battalions.

Grand total . . 93,000

N.B.—The I. Army worked in divisions, not
in corps.

II. Army, under the Crown Prince (Chief of
Staff, Blumenthal), included:

I. Corps under Bonin:

	Batts.	Squads.	Guns
I. Infantry Division . . .	13	5	24
II. ,, ,, . . .	12	4	24
Reserve Cavalry Brigade, under Bredow	—	12	6
Reserve Artillery . . .	—	—	42

Guard Corps, under Prince of Würtemberg:

I. Infantry Division . . .	13	4	24
II. ,, ,, . . .	13	4	24
I. Heavy Cavalry Brigade . .	—	8	6
Reserve Artillery . . .	—	—	30

V. Corps under Steinmetz:

IX. Infantry Division . .	10	5	24
X. ,, ,, . .	12	4	24
Reserve Artillery . . .	—	—	42

VI. Corps :

	Batts.	Squads.	Guns
XI. Infantry Division . .	12	4	18
XII. ,, ,, . .	7	4	12
Reserve Cavalry . . .	—	4	—
Reserve Artillery . . .	—	—	30
Cavalry Division, Hartmann .	—	24	12
Total	92	82	342

(234 guns being rifled), and 4 engineer battalions.

Grand total . . 115,000

Elbe Army under Herwarth von Bittenfeld, included :

	Batts.	Squads.	Guns
XIV. Infantry Division . .	13	4	24
Cavalry Brigade	—	9	—
VIII. Corps :			
XV. Infantry Division . .	12	5	24
XVI. ,, ,, . . .	13	—	12
Reserve Cavalry Brigade . .	—	8	6
Reserve Artillery	—	—	78
Total	38	26	144

and 1½ engineer battalions.

Grand total . . 46,000

I. Reserve Corps under Mülbe :

	Batts.	Squads.	Guns
Landwehr Infantry Division . .	12	—	—
Guard Landwehr	12	8	12
Landwehr Cavalry Division . .	—	16	12
Reserve Artillery. . . .	—	—	30
Total	24	24	54

Grand total . . 24,000

II. Reserve Corps :

It took no part in the operations.

Total of all the Prussian Armies . 278,000

In this account Roman figures indicate Prussians, Arabic figures indicate Austrians.

The Prussian Corps belonged to the Provinces as follows :

I. E. Prussia, II. Pomerania, III. Brandenburg, IV. Prussian Saxony, V. Posen, VI. Silesia, VII. Westphalia, VIII. Rhenish Provinces, and Guards Berlin.

CHAPTER IV

THE THEATRE

BOHEMIA is surrounded by the Böhmer Wald, Erz (Iron) Mountains, Sudetic Mountains—which are the Riesen (Giant) Mountains, the Owl Mountains, and the Glatz Hills; on the south lie the Moravian Hills. It is a strong bastion of Austria and easily defended owing to forests, mountains, and the Elbe and its tributaries. The chief passes are Schandau (closed by the Saxon fortress Königstein), Schluckenau, Reichenberg, Trautenau, Braunau, Nachod. The fortresses were: Austrian, Krakau (Cracow), Olmütz, Josephstadt, Königgrätz, Prague, Theresienstadt; Prussian, Neisse, Glatz, Kosel, Torgau. A useful distance to remember is Prague—Gitschin, 50 miles.

The railways: in Saxony the centre is Dresden, whence the Elbe line runs to Leipzig, with a western branch to Chemnitz and an eastern branch to Görlitz. During the war the chief rails used were :

A. Northern: Oderberg, Oppeln, Breslau, Dresden.

B. Southern: Prerau, Olmütz, Pardubitz, Prague; with cross lines—*e.g.*,

1. Dresden, Königstein, Theresienstadt, Prague (closed by the two fortresses).

2. Görlitz, Turnau, Prague.

3. Oderberg, Prerau.

In Bohemia is the quadrilateral of rails—Prague, Turnau, Josephstadt, Pardubitz.

Vienna had a railway to Lundenburg, whence one line ran to Prerau and another to Pardubitz. The Austrian railways were inferior to the Prussian. Telegraphs skirted all the lines.

CHAPTER V

OPERATIONS UP TO JUNE 22

Map
No. I.
Maps IV.
and V.
in Glü-
nicke.

ON May 31, Italy, all Germany and Austria were on war footing, and on June 15 a state of war existed between Prussia and Saxony, assisted by Hanover and Hesse-Kassel, and on June 20 between Prussia, Italy and their allies on the one part, and Austria, Bavaria and their allies on the other part. There was no formal declaration of war. The numbers stood—278,000 Prussians *v.* 271,000 Austrians and Saxons, 84,000 Austrians *v.* 146,000 Italians, 48,000 Prussians *v.* 120,000 of the smaller states.

Austrians as well as Prussians did not want to seem to push on war. The Bavarians were not really anxious to join the Austrian Army, and financial weakness forced the defensive on Austria, but the original concentration should have been nearer Saxony.

Austria ordered mobilisation at the end of March, and early in June the mass of the Austrian Northern Army was in Moravia, General Benedek's head-quarters at Olmütz, and Army Corps thus: in advance on the N.E., 2nd Light Cavalry

Division at Troppau; on the front Zwittau-
Zittau(Littau)-Prerau, 2nd Corps, 4th Corps,
6th Corps, and 2nd Reserve Cavalry Division; in
second line, 1st Reserve Cavalry Division and
3rd Reserve Cavalry Division N.E. of Brünn,
and the 3rd, 8th, and 10th Corps S.E. of Brünn.
The 1st Corps and 1st Light Cavalry Division
were in N. Bohemia, waiting for the Saxons.
This strategic concentration was faulty (compare
the Austrians in 1805 and the French in 1809);
if they had assembled in Bohemia they could have
acted against the dispersed Prussians, but they
never expected to be ready first.   As it was they
should have fallen on the Crown Prince.

June 17 the Saxons (24,000) moved into
Bohemia, and Benedek was informed that the
mass of the Prussians was on the Elbe; he therefore decided on his second plan, i.e. adopt Krizmanic's idea and occupy the Josephstadt-Miletin
position, covering his right with the 2nd Light
Cavalry Division.   If his information had been
correct he should have invaded Silesia.

He marched thus: on the extreme right 2nd
Light Cavalry Division and the 2nd Corps, on the
right viâ Reichenau 1st Reserve Cavalry Division,
10th Corps, 4th Corps, 6th Corps; in the centre,
viâ Wildenschwerdt, 3rd Reserve Cavalry Division
and 3rd Corps and 8th Corps; on the left on
Josephstadt 2nd Reserve Cavalry Division and
Reserve Artillery.   On June 21 Clam Gallas

(1st Corps) was directed to concentrate his corps and the Saxons near Jung Bunzlau, for Benedek was then evolving his third plan, *i.e.* to assemble all his troops on the R. Iser against the I. Army, merely holding with a weak force the Crown Prince in Silesia.

The Prussian mobilisation was ordered on May 12, though it was of no use to concentrate corps so far from the theatre of operations. The Prussian staff's excuse is that they did not then know who the enemy would be. They did know. For this purpose railways, then used for the first time on a large scale in European war (as also telegraphs and breech-loaders), were availed of. The railways terminated at Zeitz (S. of Leipzig), Halle, Herzberg (N.E. of Torgau), Görlitz, Schweidnitz, Neisse—that meant concentration on an arc of 276 miles. In these initial movements, five railways in twenty-one days carried 197,000 men, 55,000 horses, and 5,300 vehicles —contrast the railway work in 1870 and in 1904, but also contrast it with the Austrian mobilisation, which began ten weeks earlier and was not completed so soon.

The first orders were : VI. Corps to Neisse, V. Corps to Schweidnitz, Cavalry Division in rear, III. Corps to Kottbus, IV. Corps to Torgau, Guard in Berlin, VII. and VIII. Corps in the west. In a few days Moltke saw the Austrians and Saxons would be the main objective, and therefore moved the XIV. Division and VIII. Corps eastwards. On the Bohemian re-entrant, theory advised a concentration on Görlitz, but that meant time, and therefore two separate concentrations (with all their dangers) took place to cover Berlin and Silesia.

On May 14 Moltke reported he could begin invasion on June 5 with 270,000 men, but the King declined such vigorous action. On May 16 the II. Corps was ordered to Herzberg, and thus was formed the I. Army under Frederick Charles, the "Red Prince." The II. Army consisted of the V. and VI. Corps and Cavalry Division under the Crown Prince near Neisse; its duty was to protect Silesia, for which purpose also two detached forces under Knoblesdorf and Stolberg were posted near Oderberg, E. of Troppau. The Guard and I. Corps were held back at first. Next the I. Corps moved to Görlitz as a link between the I. and II. Armies, whilst the VIII. Corps entrained to Halle and the XIV. Division to Zeitz —these last two forces would be the Army of the Elbe under Herwarth von Bittenfeld. At Berlin also was the I. Reserve Corps of Landwehr under Mülbe (24,000 strong).

Map I. in Bonnal.

Moltke saw this wide arc of concentration was too dangerous, and therefore on May 30 he issued orders to ensure closer union, which orders were executed by June 10. The V. and VI. Corps moved to Landshut, the Cavalry Division in rear;

Map I. in Bonnal.

II., III., IV. Corps closed south-eastwards on
Görlitz, and the Elbe Army shifted to Torgau.
The I. Corps (added to II. Army on June 4)
marched from Görlitz to Landshut; Frederick
Charles objected to this strengthening of the
II. Army. The arc of concentration was still
156 miles.

Before Prussia could deal with Austria she
must secure her rear against Hanover and Hesse-
Kassel, which also cut her off from Westphalia
and Rhenish Prussia. Therefore on June 16
Prussia invaded Hanover, and the Hanoverian
Army, after the useless victory of Langensalza,
N. of Gotha, had to surrender on June 29. Hesse-
Kassel was overrun, her troops retiring south.

Meantime on June 11 some spy had given
Prussia full information as to the Austrians.
Moltke feared Herwarth was not equal to the
Saxons and the Austrian 1st Corps, and so he
gave him Mülbe from Berlin; he also feared
Benedek would invade Silesia, and so com-
mitted the errors of adding the Guards to the
II. Army and of allowing the Crown Prince to
return to Neisse. Besides, the King and the
Crown Prince urged the necessity of protecting
Silesia, and Moltke yielded to them and issued
the June 12 orders, which were executed by
Map III. June 18. Under these orders the II. Army
in Bon-
nal. returned to its old positions—viz. VI. Corps,
V. Corps, and I. Corps from Landshut to Neisse,

Cavalry Division in rear, Guards from Berlin to Brieg (N. of Neisse). Total of II. Army, 115,000. The assignment of the Guards to the II. Army was objectionable to Frederick Charles; in the I. Army (93,000 strong), the III. and IV. and II. Corps moved into the front, Landshut-Görlitz, Cavalry Corps in rear; the Elbe Army (46,000) could not move because Saxony was in the way, but in order to strengthen it Mülbe's force at Berlin went to Torgau, raising Herwarth to 70,000.

The arc of concentration then was 208 miles, and a march into Saxony became necessary in order to unite the Elbe and I. Armies, to open the Chemnitz line (Chemnitz, S.W. of Dresden), to secure the Bohemian passes, and to isolate the Bavarians from the Austrians. Therefore on June 16 the Elbe Army invaded Saxony, entering Dresden June 18, and next day the Elbe Army was placed under Frederick Charles. Mülbe's troops stopped in Saxony, except the Guard Landwehr, which moved with the rest of the Elbe Army. The I. Army also on June 16 entered Saxony, and reached the following positions by June 22 : VII. and VIII. Divisions Map IV. in Bonal. Plan on Zittau, III. and IV. in rear, V. and VI. on the left, Cavalry Corps in rear. The army was p. 78 in Glünicke. on a very wide front.

On June 22 Moltke issued the important order assigning Gitschin (Jicin) as the point of junction

3

of the I. and II. Armies, but for the present the
VI. Corps was to halt at Neisse. General Bonnal
says Königinhof was a better point of concentration, as being more central, and indeed on
June 29 the I. Army was ordered to pass beyond
Gitschin. To choose some point of concentration
in Bohemia was necessary in order to repair the
previous error of separation.

CHAPTER VI

OPERATIONS ON THE R. ISER, JUNE 23—29

ON June 23 the Elbe Army and the I. Army Map IV. in Bonnal. Plan p. 78 in Glünicke. invaded Bohemia, whilst Benedek's main body was still moving on Josephstadt. The I. Army made for Reichenberg, the Elbe Army for Rumburg; opposed were 60,000 of the Saxons, and 1st Corps and 1st Light Cavalry Division, collected on the left bank of the Iser, between Turnau and Jung-Bunzlau.

On June 24 the Saxon Crown Prince (in command of 1st Corps and of Saxons) was ordered by Map IV. in Bonnal. Plan p. 78 in Glünicke. Benedek "to oppose the Prussians," who this day were : I. Army on Gablonz, cavalry in rear, the VIII. Corps and XIV. Division of Elbe Army on Gabel.

On June 25 Frederick Charles halted the I. Army round Reichenberg and Gablonz, cavalry still in rear, in order to fetch up the Elbe Army, Map V. in Bonnal. which was closing on Gabel, Guard Landwehr Division in rear.

Consequently, on June 26, Herwarth pushed his XIV. Division to Oschotz and VIII. Corps to Niemes, with advanced guard to Hühnerwasser. This led to the action of Hühnerwasser, whence

35

some Austrian outposts were driven back. Meantime the VII. Division moved to Turnau, and the VIII. Division on Podol, skirmishing at Liebenau with the Light Cavalry Division. On reaching Turnau, Fransecky (VII. Division) repaired the bridge and threw a pontoon, and Frederick Charles should then have pushed from this place straight on to Gitschin.

The VIII. Division meantime brought on the

Podol,
June 26.
Plan
No. II.
Plan VI.
in Glü-
niche.

ACTION OF PODOL, June 26.

The VIII. Division moved on this place, crossed the river and drove the Austrians out. Then, at 9.30 p.m., a brigade of the Austrian 1st Corps drove the Prussians back over the river, and at 11 p.m. the Prussian officer decided to retire. But Brigadier-General Bose, with two fresh battalions, renewed the struggle. Austrian counter attacks were delivered in column formation, which were foiled by volleys at thirty yards. The Prussians then carried the main bridge with the bayonet, and, in spite of Austrian reinforcements, under Clam Gallas, they took the other bridge also. The action ceased at 1 a.m.

Comments : (1) Deadly nature of the Prussian fire ; (2) Excellent conduct of Bose ; (3) The strategic advantages of seizing the Podol bridges were that they opened the short route to Gitschin, rendered Turnau safe, and threatened the junction of the Saxon Crown Prince with Benedek.

The ill success of the Allies was partly due to Benedek's contradictory telegrams to the Saxon Crown Prince—at 2 p.m., "Hold Münchengrätz and Turnau at all costs"; at 10 p.m., "Leave it to your discretion"—and partly to the fact that Clam Gallas disobeyed the Prince's order to hold Turnau. He thus resigned the Iser passage. The fact is that the Saxon Prince did not use his cavalry to scout. That night the Elbe Army was N.W. of Münchengrätz, I. Army on Podol and Turnau, cavalry still in rear, and the Saxon Crown Prince at Münchengrätz. Map VI. in Bonnal.

On June 27 the I. Army closed up towards the VII. and VIII. Divisions, the V. Division reaching the Iser above Turnau, and the Elbe Army closed in on the right of the I. Army. This day the Map VII. in Bonnal. Allies decided to retire their main body from Münchengrätz next day. Frederick Charles, convinced they would hold fast, directed the Elbe Army straight on Münchengrätz, whilst Tümpling's V. Division was to threaten the enemy's right viâ Rowensko.

ACTION ON MÜNCHENGRÄTZ, June 28

Frederick Charles supposed that the Saxons and two Austrian Corps were at Münchengrätz. He also supposed they would stand there all the 28th, as a fact they retired early, leaving only rear-guards. On the Austrian side, the Saxon Crown Prince had, on June 26 at 2 p.m., a telegram from Münchengrätz, June 28. Plan No. II. Plan VI. in Glünicke.

Benedek, "Hold Turnau and Münchengrätz at all costs"; therefore he decided to stand firm on the 27th, but then on the 26th at 10 p.m. came a telegram giving him discretion and implying merely a retarding action.

The Elbe Army at 10 a.m. attacked Clam Gallas' rearguard, forced it across the Iser R. and from the Musky Berg. Tümpling's V. Division's advance from the north also had its effect. Losses were far fewer on the Prussian side.

Comments : (1) Frederick Charles should have acted on the 27th; (2) Clam Gallas should on the 27th have driven the few Prussians at Turnau and at Podol over the R. Iser, then clung to Münchengrätz, then retired only to Sobotka and not to Gitschin.

The positions in the evening were—I. Army S. of the Iser R., on the front Münchengrätz-Rowensko, cavalry in rear N. of the river, Elbe Army at Münchengrätz, Guard Landwehr far in rear, and the Saxons and 1st Corps at Sobotka, and the 1st Light Cavalry Division at Gitschin, whither the two corps were moving.

On June 29 Frederick Charles brought on the

Map VIII. in Bonnal.

BATTLE OF GITSCHIN, June 29

Gitschin, June 29. Plan No. III. Plan X. in Glü-nicke.

The Prussians moved thus : V. Division, IV. Division, and I. Cavalry Division along the Turnau road; III., VII., VI. Divisions and Reserve Artillery along the Sobotka road; VIII.

Division and II. Cavalry Division *viâ* Bautzen.
Elbe Army was kept on the R. Iser at München-
chengrätz. Of all these, only 26,000 men took
part in the battle against 42,000 Austrians.
Clam Gallas, in the Saxon prince's temporary
absence, occupied the Gitschin position with the
Saxons and 1st Corps: Left at Lochow, Centre
on the heights of Prachow and Brada, Right at
Eisenstadtl, with Cavalry Division and Reserve
Artillery at Diletz; Reserve behind Brada. On
the extreme left were the Saxons at Podhrad.
At 7 a.m. Frederick Charles had orders from
Berlin to push rapidly on past Gitschin (the
original rendezvous) so as to help the II. Army.
He therefore ordered the movement on Gitschin.

Tümpling's V. Division arriving, contained the
Austrian centre and captured Diletz on the
Austrian right, which, however, the Saxons
passing through Gitschin recaptured. At that
moment came Benedek's order to avoid battle
with superior forces and to retire on Horitz
and Miletin to connect with main army. The
Saxon Crown Prince ordered a retreat.

On the Austrian left, Werder's III. Division
attacked with success, and late at night the
III. and V. Divisions entered Gitschin. The
Allies in confusion retreated to Horitz, Miletin,
and Smidar. Losses far greater on the Austrian
side. .

Comments: (1) Austrians and Saxons should

PODOL & MÜNCHENGRÄTZ
June 26, 28.

Theatre, Woody & Hilly.

Scale :
Münchengrätz − Musky Berg. 3 miles.

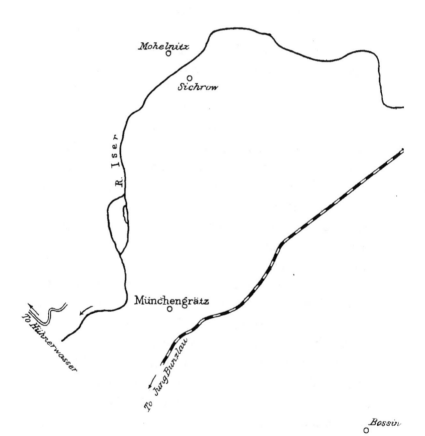

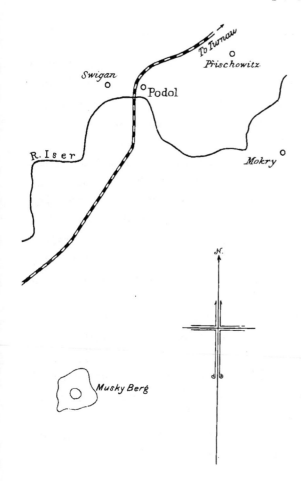

have massed S.E. of Gitschin, holding that town and watching the roads leading to it, and then acted in mass against the approaching Prussian columns; (2) The Crown Prince should not have retired on Benedek's order; he should have won the battle, as he could have done; his retreat was badly managed; (3) On the Prussian side Frederick Charles engaged only 26,000, and the two divisions belonged to different corps. The fact is that he disliked the corps organisation and had foolishly abolished it in his army. He had had too many men at Münchengrätz, and if he had marched rapidly to Gitschin he could have severed the Saxon Crown Prince from Benedek. He had kept his cavalry back.

Map IX. in Bonnal.

The positions on the evening were: I. Army on Gitschin, which its leading divisions occupied (III. and V.), cavalry still in rear, Elbe Army at Münchengrätz, Saxon Crown Prince in retreat. Note that Gitschin was a temporary strategic point; compare Quatre Bras, 1815.

GITSCHIN
June 29

Scale
Gitschin-Brada 2 miles

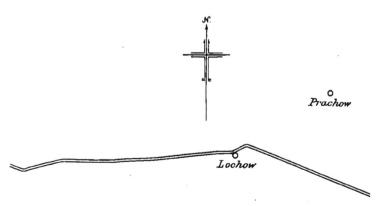

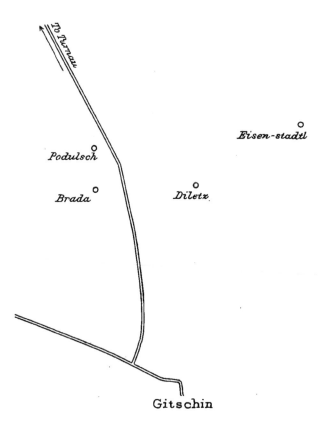

CHAPTER VII

OPERATIONS ON THE UPPER ELBE, JUNE 23—29

TO assist the passage of the II. Army through the mountains the VI. Corps at Neisse was to feint and then to march to Glatz to cover the Crown Prince's rear. This feint had the effect of causing Benedek to keep back his 2nd Corps. By June 25 the I. Corps was at Libau (Cavalry Map V. Division in rear), Guards at Neurode, V. Corps _{in Bon-} nal. and VI. Corps near Glatz.

On June 26 the V. Corps and the Guards Plan started, and on the 27th the I. Corps and Cavalry ^{p. 70} Division; the VI. Corps was to follow the _{nicke.} V. Corps. There was not much danger, because the Guards could support either wing. But three errors interfered with the safety of the movement—(1) on account of a rumour the Crown Prince halted the VI. Corps at Habelschwerdt June 27, so that it lost time; (2) Bonin's foolish retirement after the Trautenau action; (3) the Guard Cavalry was not used to scout—in fact, all the cavalry was little used; therefore on June 28 Benedek had a good chance.

That night (the 26th) the II. Army stood thus:

Map VI. in Bonnal. I. Corps and Cavalry Division at Libau, Guards on Braunau Pass, V. Corps on Nachod Pass, VI. Corps at Glatz. It should be noted that the Austrian maps did not show Braunau Pass.

On the Austrian side Benedek was moving on Josephstadt, and by the 25th his six corps and four cavalry divisions stretched from Josephstadt back to Zwittau, the 1st Reserve Cavalry Division being at Skalitz, and the three other cavalry divisions in rear, the 10th Corps at Josephstadt, and 4th, 6th, and 8th Corps behind in the order stated. On June 26th the Austrian cavalry reported the Crown Prince's march, and Benedek could have used against him all his corps except the 2nd Corps. His positions that Plan p. 84 in Glünicke. night were: 10th Corps at Königinhof on Trautenau, 4th Corps at Josephstadt, 1st Reserve Cavalry Division at Skalitz, 6th and 8th Corps behind these forces and 3rd Corps on the left of the 6th and 8th Corps, the 2nd Corps and the three other Cavalry Divisions and the Reserve Artillery still in rear. The Austrian commander did not profit by this position to attack the Crown Prince; he was bent on moving his mass against the I. Army (his third plan), and therefore directed only the 10th Corps on Trautenau and the 6th Corps and 1st Reserve Cavalry Division on Nachod, that is a mere containing force.

On June 27 the movements led to two actions,
Trautenau and Nachod.

ACTION OF TRAUTENAU, JUNE 27

Bonin's I. Corps from Libau started for
Trautenau at 4 a.m., and occupied the place in
the morning. But then appeared an Austrian
brigade of the 10th Corps on the Galgenberg ; the
Prussian advanced guard could not move them,
and at 11.30 a.m. Bonin detailed 5 battalions and
1 battery under Gen. Buddenbrock against the
enemy's eastern flank, whilst the advanced guard
pressed on in front. The latter drove back the
Austrians before Buddenbrock arrived at 1 p.m.
His flank attack on the retreating Austrians was
less effective because Bonin at that moment retired
half his advanced guard on Trautenau. At 3 p.m.,
however, the Prussians occupied the front Hohen-
bruck-Alt Rognitz, whilst the Austrian brigade
fell back to Neu Rognitz.

Traute-
nau,
June 27.
Plan
No. IV.
Plan VII.
in Glü-
nicke.

At 1 p.m. the I. Guard Infantry Division
marching on Eipel (on the R. Aupa) could
have helped Bonin, but he declined, and they
went on to Eipel. But at 3.30 p.m., when the
other half of the advanced guard had by error
been recalled to Trautenau, the left (eastern)
flank of Buddenbrock was assailed by another
Austrian brigade and his front by the original
brigade from Neu Rognitz. At 4 p.m. he retreated,
especially as a third Austrian brigade arrived.

Consequently at 4.30 p.m. all the Prussians retired from Trautenau towards Parschnitz (Pranochnitz); and when at 6.30 p.m. a fourth Austrian brigade moved from Alt Rognitz, Bonin ordered a general retreat in the night over the mountains to his original starting-point—a retreat quite needless, as the Austrians did not pursue. The numbers were: Austrians, 33,000 and 72 guns; Prussians, 35,000 and 96 guns. Prussian losses were far fewer.

Comments: (1) Bonin's leading very bad; he had kept his cavalry back; he (unlike Steinmetz at Nachod) did not rapidly seize a dominating point securing the issue of the defile; he sent in his troops piecemeal and engaged less than half his force; his guns were held back; he foolishly retired his advanced guard; (2) He could on retiring have halted at Parschnitz and either waited for the Guards or renewed the attack next day; nor did he report his retreat to the Crown Prince; (3) As to the Austrians, they used the bayonet and hardly any fire-preparation, hence their great losses. Gen. Gablenz (10th Corps) took up a forward position, unlike Ramming at Nachod, who took up a position in rear of that place; but even Gablenz could gain little because Benedek would not permit pursuit across the frontier; (4) The Prussian failure to seize early the Galgenberg heights was due to the divisional commander waiting at Parschnitz in strict conformity with orders; contrast the initiative displayed by Baron Constant de Rebecque at Quatre Bras, 1815; Adams in " Great Campaigns " defends the divisional commander's action.

ACTION OF NACHOD, June 27.

Gen. Ramming with the 6th Corps, 28,000 Nachod, infantry, the 1st Reserve Cavalry Division (4,000 June 27, Plan horse), 88 guns, moved from Opocno on Skalitz; No. V. Plan he would meet Steinmetz's V. Corps, 22,000 VIII. in Glü- infantry, 2,000 horse, 90 guns. The leading nicke. Austrian brigade at 7.30 a.m. reached Sonow (Schonow) to find in front Steinmetz's advanced guard. Then another Austrian brigade came up at 9.30 a.m. on that brigade's left, north of Sonow, and a third Austrian brigade still more to the north near Prowodow (Promodow). The Corps Artillery did not reach Skalitz till 11 a.m. The Prussians were hard pressed along the Neustadt road, though some of their cavalry by a charge drove some Austrian horse back on Kleny and broke some infantry.

About noon the X. Division arrived and attacked the left wing of the brigade near Prowodow and repulsed the fourth Austrian brigade, which came up from Kleny at 2 p.m., and an hour later Gen. Ramming retreated on Skalitz. Losses: Austrian, 8 guns, and in men far more than the Prussians.

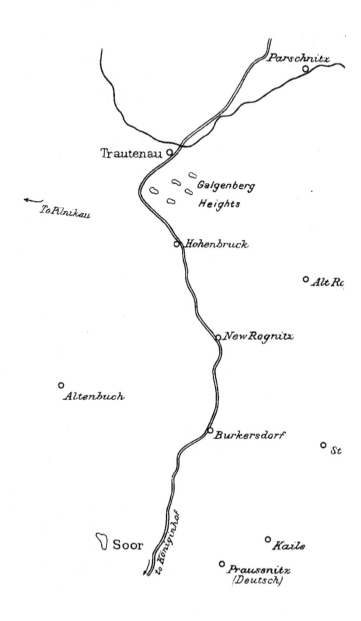

Parschnitz

Trautenau

Galgenberg
Heights

To Pilnikau

Hohenbruck

Alt Ro

New Rognitz

Altenbuch

Burkersdorf

St

Soor

to Königinhof

Kaile

Praussnitz
(Deutsch)

TRAUTENAU & SOOR (BURKERSDORF)
June 27-28

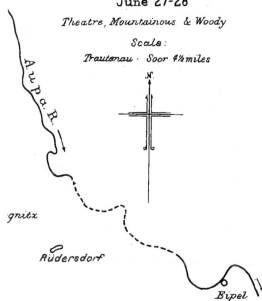

Theatre, Mountainous & Woody

Scale:

Trautenau · Soor 4½ miles

gnitz

Rüdersdorf

Eipel

zudenz

Comments : (1) Steinmetz should have pursued ; (2) The Austrians fought disconnectedly : they were inferior at rifle fire, and not superior with the bayonet. They attacked in battalion-columns of double companies, used no fire-preparation, and relied on the bayonet. The leading brigade should have gone *viá* Sonow against the Prussian flank, whilst the other brigades opposed the enemy in front.

On the same day occurred the combat of Oswiecim on the frontier of upper Silesia in west Galicia, where a Prussian raid was repulsed.

Map VII. in Bonnal. The positions that night were: II. Army, I. Corps and Cavalry Division at Libau, Guards at Eipel, V. and part of the VI. between Nachod and Skalitz, part of VI. S.W. of Glatz ; Austrians, 10th Corps south of Trautenau, 6th Corps and 1st Reserve Cavalry Division south of Skalitz, 4th and 8th Corps at Josephstadt, 3rd Corps at Miletin, the rest in rear.

On June 28 two more actions took place, Soor and Skalitz.

ACTION OF SOOR (BURKERSDORF), June 28

Soor (Burkersdorf), June 28. Plan No. IV. Plan VII. in Glünicke. To assist the I. Corps the Guards were directed on June 28 through Eipel towards Kaile, the Crown Prince being ignorant of Bonin's retreat. On the Austrian side General Gablenz (10th Corps) was after his victory at Trautenau, ordered to return on Praussnitz and to form there facing east. This was unwise; it would have been better to have drawn back the 10th Corps, after its losses, on Königinhof: and on the Prussian side the Crown Prince should have hurried in person to Burkersdorf.

Gablenz began to retire his four brigades on Praussnitz. This movement being reported to the Prince of Würtemberg (commanding the Guards), he foolishly ordered his advanced guard to fall back behind the R. Aupa and then waited to connect with the I. Corps, though his orders were to move on Kaile. At 9 a.m., however, he advanced on Burkersdorf, whence at 11.30 a.m. the Guards drove one Austrian brigade and their corps artillery back to Altenbuch; they were joined there by two other brigades, and all then retired on Pilnikau. Meantime, the fourth brigade (left in ignorance) marching through Rüdersdorf was heavily attacked by the Prussian Guards, and with difficulty and heavy loss reached Pilnikau. As usual the Prussian losses were fewer, and the Austrian prisoners numerous.

Comments : (1) If the Guards had not delayed and had pushed forward cavalry, the 10th Corps would have been captured ; (2) If Benedek had supported the 10th Corps with another corps he could have crushed the Guards. Gablenz had reported his danger from the Guards, and, at first, part of the 4th Corps was ordered by Benedek to

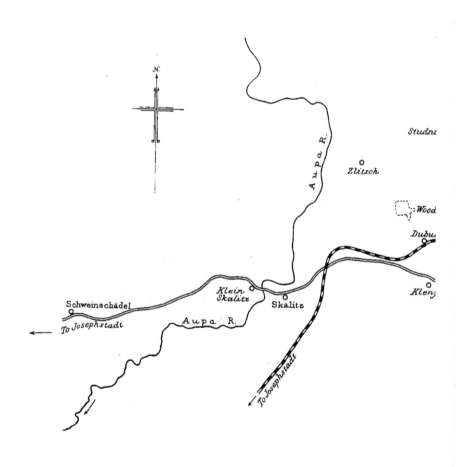

NACHOD, SKALITZ & SCHWEINSCHÄDEL
June 27, 28, 29.

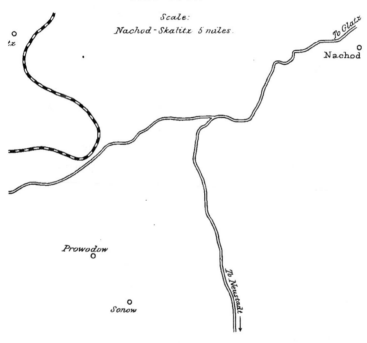

Scale:
Nachod - Skalitz 5 miles.

To Glatz

Nachod

tz

Prowodow

Sonow

To Neustadt

In east, mountains;
In west, woods.

occupy Praussnitz near Kaile to cover Gablenz's right against the Guards. This force was counter-manded without Gablenz's knowledge; hence his defeat.

ACTION OF SKALITZ, JUNE 28

Skalitz, June 28, Plan No. V. Plan VIII. in Glü-nicke.

Benedek had sent the 8th Corps to relieve the 6th Corps (both under Archduke Leopold); the 4th Corps also came up from Josephstadt. At 10.20 a.m. Benedek in person reached Skalitz and directed Leopold to retire at once. The Austrian 8th Corps was at that time posted at Skalitz, holding 2,500 yards, *i.e.* 8 men per yard; the R. Aupa in rear, and just in front of the left wing a wood. They should have been on the western bank of the river.

The Archduke then ordered a battalion to reconnoitre the Dubno wood and thus caused the undesired battle. On the Prussian side Steinmetz (V. Corps) had orders to take Skalitz; he was reinforced by one brigade of the VI. Corps and by the Guard Cuirassiers. He moved troops to Studnitz so as to connect with the Guards. The rest of his force marched along the Kleny road. Both bodies soon after 11 a.m. rushed into the Dubno wood and nearly annihilated the single Austrian battalion there. The corps batteries at Kleny tackled the Austrian guns at Skalitz. The Austrians vainly tried to resist, but had to retire towards Skalitz, whilst Prussian rifles, having crossed the bridge near Zlitsch, approached Klein-Skalitz. Losses were as usual more numerous on the Austrian side, and the Prussians had secured the Gates of Bohemia.

Comments: (1) Leopold was incapable, provoked the contest, and could not handle his troops; (2) The Austrians were of different nationalities; (3) Their cavalry should have discovered the Prussian advance, and as usual they employed battalion-columns and relied on the bayonet; (4) The Austrian left should have held the heights behind Zlitsch, the right Skalitz, and the ridge to Zlitsch should have been enfiladed by guns at Skalitz; (5) The Prussians did not connect with the Guards and did not pursue.

The positions this night were: II. Army, I. Corps and Cavalry Division at Libau, Guards at Traute-nau, V. and part of VI. at Skalitz, part of the VI. S.W. of Glatz. Austrians: 4th Corps and 1st Reserve Cavalry Division at Dolan (between Skalitz and Josephstadt), 10th Corps W. of Pilnikau, 3rd Corps, 6th Corps, 8th Corps, 2nd Corps, and 2nd Light Cavalry Division on the front, Miletin-Josephstadt, 2nd and 3rd Reserve Cavalry Divisions in second line. It should be noted that the Guard Cuirassiers left Steinmetz and rejoined the Guard. This night the Crown Prince heard that the I. Corps was at Libau, and decided to concentrate the next day his whole army at Königinhof, and consequently the

Map VIII. in Bonnal.

4

detached part of the VI. Corps was ordered to
join Steinmetz.

On this day Benedek had another good chance
against the Crown Prince, but at 8 p.m. he learnt
of Gablenz's defeat at Soor, and thus knew he
could not march against the I. Army; he formed
then his fourth plan—to accept battle in the
Dubenetz position. On June 29 the II. Army moved with Königinhof as its objective, and the Guards, on their
advance, drove the retreating 10th Corps out of
Königinhof, and at the same time occurred the

ACTION OF SCHWEINSCHÄDEL, June 29

Schwein-
schädel,
June 29.
Plan
No. V.
Plan
VIII.
in Glü-
nicke.

Here the V. Corps plus the XXII. brigade of
VI. Corps and the Heavy Cavalry of the Guard
engaged the 4th Corps. Steinmetz (V. Corps)
wanted to march to Gradlitz to join the Guards
and the I. Corps, and for this purpose to go *viâ*
Zlitsch round the left of the 4th Corps. He was
reinforced by the rest of the VI. Corps, and thus
had 50,000 men. He should then have crushed
the 4th Corps and driven it over the Elbe, but
he was bent on his flank march. In this march
he struck the Austrian outposts, and the resulting
struggle led to a Prussian movement against
Schweinschädel. The place fell, but the victorious
troops were foolishly recalled by Steinmetz, who
thereupon resumed his move on Gradlitz. The

4th Corps crossed the Elbe to Salnei. Losses as usual.

The Armies held the following positions at night : II. Army, I. Corps at Pilnikau, Cavalry Division at Praussnitz near Kaile, Guard at Königinhof, V. and VI. Corps at Gradlitz. Austrians, in the Dubenetz position facing north, on the front Miletin-Josephstadt, in first line 3rd Corps, two Cavalry Divisions, 6th Corps, 10th Corps, and 2nd Corps, in second line on the right 8th and 4th Corps and two Cavalry Divisions, Artillery Reserve in rear.

Map IX. in Bonnal.

CHAPTER VIII

OPERATIONS PRECEDING THE BATTLE OF KÖNIGGRÄTZ, JUNE 30—JULY 2

ON June 30 the I. and II. Armies connected by cavalry at Arnau at 12.30 p.m. King William arrived with Moltke, whilst on the Austrian side the 1st Corps reached Sadowa in a terrible condition, and the Saxons reached Smidar together with the 1st Light Cavalry Division; and at night the army still held the Dubenetz position. Benedek,

Map X. in Bonnal. knowing his losses, and that the I. and II. and Elbe Armies were converging on him, formed a fifth plan, *i.e.* retreat on Königgrätz by a night march. He would probably have done better to cross the Elbe and stand between Josephstadt and Königgrätz.

That night the Prussian positions were: Elbe Army S.W. of Gitschin, I. Army E. of Gitschin; II. Army — I. Corps at Pilnikau, Guards at Königinhof, V. and VI. Corps at Gradlitz, cavalry division in rear.

On July 1, at 1 a.m., the disorderly retreat

Map XI. in Bonnal. began on Königgrätz, and Benedek telegraphed to the Emperor, urging peace at any price. The Emperor declined, and Benedek replied he would rest the troops on July 2, and probably then retire on Olmütz. The Prussians failed to follow this retreat with cavalry, and actually were ignorant that Benedek's main army had ever occupied the Dubenetz position, and now supposed he was behind the Elbe. That night the Saxons from Smidar and all the Austrians were behind the Bistritz R. The Prussian II. Army remained as before, except that the I. Corps crossed the Elbe to Praussnitz, the I. Army had pushed as far as Miletin and Horitz, the Elbe Army on Smidar. This was not very vigorous, but the French Ambassador had reached headquarters, and politics made themselves felt.

July 2: the I. and II. Armies would have joined this day, but Moltke kept them separate, and moved the Elbe Army southward, so as to get its manœuvre interval. Telegraphic communication with the II. Army failed, and this nearly ruined Moltke's combination. Indeed, if telegraphic communication had been kept up, the I. Army would not have attacked so early. This telegraphic failure reflects badly on Prussian management, and indeed the result was that the fate of the battle hung on one officer carrying the decisive order to the II. Army.

The Prussian positions were: Right, Elbe Army on Smidar; Centre, I. Army on Horitz; Left, II. Army—I. Corps W. of Elbe at Praussnitz; E. of Elbe Cavalry Division at Arnau or Plan XII. in Glünicke, and Map XII. in Bonnal.

Neustadt, Guards at Königinhof, V. and VI.
Corps at Gradlitz.

Neither side knew much of the other, and the
Prussians supposed Benedek was on the left of
the Elbe between Königgrätz and Josephstadt.
Moltke, therefore, directed the Elbe Army on
Chlumetz and to secure the Pardubitz crossing;
I. Army on Horitz; II. Army—I. Corps *viâ* Miletin
to Gross Bürglitz, the rest of the Army to stop
left of the Elbe and to reconnoitre towards the
Aupa and the Mettau. The idea was, no doubt,
a concentric attack on Benedek's supposed position,
but the orders were never issued, because the
real Austrian position was ascertained. Frederick
Charles at once jumped to the conclusion that
the Austrian commander meant to attack. He
thereupon ordered the Elbe Army on Nechanitz
and the I. Army against the Austrian centre, and
practically tried to order the Crown Prince to
cover the I. Army's left with the Guards and
I. Corps at Gross Bürglitz, whilst the V. and VI.
Corps would merely observe Josephstadt. This
would have been fatal. Moltke stopped it, and
won the battle by attacking with the I. Army
and the Elbe Army, and by bringing the whole
II. Army on the Austrian right.

If the Austrians had been in the supposed
position, east of the Elbe, Moltke could either
(*a*) attack in front with the Elbe and I. Armies,
and in flank with the II. Army, or (*b*) bring the

Plan XIII. in Bonnal.

Plan XIV. in Bonnal.

II. Army to the west bank of the Elbe, and move in mass on Pardubitz, thus exccuting a dangerous flank march.

In the Austrian army, Krizmanic, chief of Operations, Henikstein, Chief of the Staff, Clam Gallas of the 1st Corps were displaced, and Baumgarten became Chief of the Staff. The best plan would have been to replace Benedek by the Archduke Albert and his Chief of Staff, Von John, who had won Custozza on June 24 in the Italian Quadrilateral. All this day the Austrians rested, and Benedek altered his mind and decided on battle (his sixth plan), though he had not fully prepared the position for defence. At 2 a.m., July 3, he gave orders for battle, stating that the Reserve was at his sole disposal, that he would be near Chlum, that the line of retreat would be *viâ* Holiz-Hohenmauth, and that Königgrätz was not to be entered.

CHAPTER IX

BATTLE OF KÖNIGGRÄTZ, JULY 3

THE Austrian positions as ordered were as follows :

Left: Saxons, Popowitz-Tresowitz; on their left, Saxon Cavalry and 1st Light Cavalry Division. In support 8th Corps, all facing W.

Centre: 10th Corps, N. of Tresowitz, facing W.; 3rd Corps, Lipa-Chlum, facing N.

Right: 4th Corps, Chlum-Nedelist; 2nd Corps, E. of Nedelist; 2nd Light Cavalry Division, S. of Nedelist, all facing N.

Reserve: At Sweti 1st and 3rd Reserve Cavalry Divisions. At Roswitz and Briza 6th and 1st Corps, 2nd Reserve Cavalry Division, and Reserve Artillery.

The actual positions taken up were:

Left: A Saxon brigade and 1st Light Cavalry Division, Lubno; Saxon Corps, Nieder Prim-Problus with Reserve Artillery of 8th Corps behind and 8th Corps to the N. of Problus; 10th Corps, W. of Langenhof.

56

Advanced troops Nechanitz to Sadowa on
other side of Bistritz R.   All facing W.

Centre : 3rd Corps, one brigade at Sadowa facing
W.; rest of 3rd Corps, 1st Reserve Cavalry
Division and half Reserve Artillery, Lipa-
Chlum, facing north.

Right : 4th Corps, Maslowed, facing N.W.;
2nd Corps, Horenowes, facing W.   Behind
it one of its own brigades on the R. Trotina
(Trotinka), and the 2nd Light Cavalry
Division on the E. bank of that river.

Reserve : Rosnitz, half Reserve Artillery ; Sweti,
3rd Reserve Cavalry Division ; Briza, 2nd
Reserve Cavalry Division; Langenhof, 1st
and 6th Corps.

Note : 8th Corps had only three brigades in the
battle ; one of these was on outpost duty at
Horenowes, and the other two were with the
Saxons.

The Bistritz, a real obstacle, was passable only
at the bridges which Benedek did not destroy,
because he fancied he might take the offensive.
Towards the west it was a strong position, and the
Prussian guns could do no good unless they got
across the river.   There were many fir-trees in
the field, and as the village houses were of wood
they were not good for defence.   Behind lay the
Elbe, unfordable as some say, with twelve bridges.
Three points were important—Horenowes, support
for the right, Chlum, link between right and

centre, Hradek, support for the left; and in the orders Horenowes was neglected. At a few points abattis and fire trenches had been made.

The numbers engaged were 215,000 Austrians and Saxons with 770 guns, and 221,000 Prussians with 780 guns, being thus the greatest of battles except those in Manchuria.

At 6 a.m. in fog and rain Frederick Charles moved his VIII. Division and II. Corps on Sadowa, V. and VI. Divisions and Reserve Artillery to support the VIII. Division, Cavalry Corps to connect with his Elbe Army as the latter moved on Nechanitz; VII. Division on the left of the VIII. Division. In the II. Army all was ready, except that the VI. Corps had not yet had its orders for Welchow. At 8 a.m. the King at Dub ordered attack, and 150 guns opened on either side.

At 8.30 a.m. the VII. Division moved on Benatek, and the VIII. Division crossed at Sowetitz, the Austrian detachment evacuating Sadowa, and by 10 a.m. all the 3rd Corps was between Lipa and Chlum, and its terrific fire drove the VIII. Division into the Hola wood. Then came the II. Corps with its 8 batteries S.W. of Mzan, III. Division E. of Dohalicka, IV. Division in the Hola wood. But at the same time the 10th Corps massed at Langenhof, whence and from Lipa and Chlum 200 guns fired till noon. It was an awful fire, and the I. Army could get only 102 guns across the Bistritz. The Sadowa bridge was the only passage possible here for guns. For four hours, 11 a.m. to 3 p.m., the Austrian guns pinned the VIII., IV., and III. Divisions.

Meantime the V. and VI. Divisions crossed the Bistritz, and thus six divisions held a line of 7,000 yards (ten men per yard); hence heavy losses, and at 1 p.m. defeat seemed certain. More to the north the VII. Division with a cavalry brigade and its four batteries acted, viâ Benatek, against the 4th Corps, whose commander, Festetic, reinforced his men in the Swiep or Maslowed wood. The Prussians attacked the wood, and as the 3rd Corps, massing at Lipa-Chlum, evacuated Cistowes, they seized that village. Then both the 4th and 2nd Corps moved against the wood and retook it after an heroic defence by Fransecky, who, with a loss of 2,000 men, fell back to Benatek at 12 noon, whilst the 4th and 2nd Corps had lost 13,000, and had also opened the road for the II. Army.

In the II. Army the Crown Prince at 5 a.m. ordered the I. Corps and Cavalry Division on Gross Burglitz, Guards on Jericek, VI. Corps on Welchow, V. Corps on Choteborek, which last place he reached himself at 11.15 a.m. and saw the danger of the VII. Division. He therefore directed the I. Division Guards and the VI. Corps on Horenowes, where were five Austrian batteries.

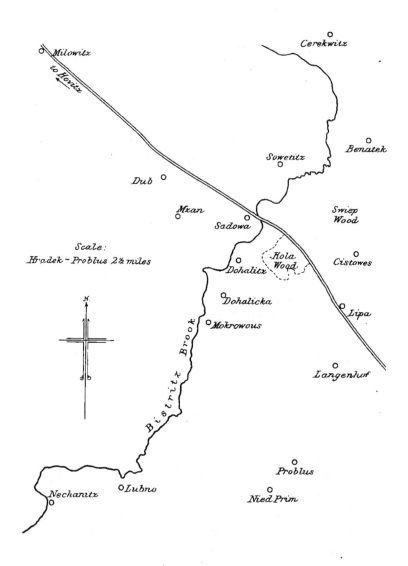

Cerekwitz

Milowitz

to Horitz

Benatek

Sowetitz

Dub

Swiep
Wood

Mzan

Sadowa

Scale:
Hradek ~ Problus 2½ miles

Hola
Wood

Cistowes

Dohalitz

N

Dohalicka

Lipa

Mokrowous

B i s t r i t z   B r o o k

Langenhof

Problus

Nechanitz

Lubno

Nied Prim

Hradek

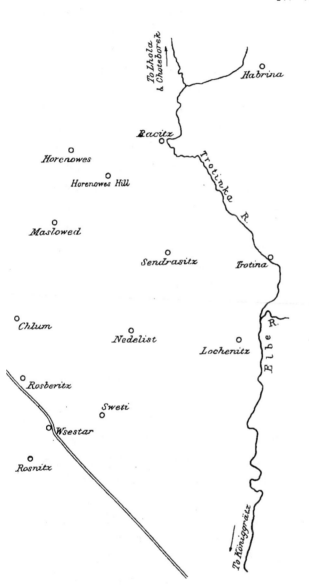

N.º VI.

At the same moment Benedek, planning a counter-attack on the I. Army, brought his Reserve (1st and 6th Corps, and 2nd and 3rd Reserve Cavalry Divisions) to Lipa and Langenhof. On Baumgarten's advice he turned the 6th Corps on Chlum and Nedelist, but at once recalled it. He then, at 11.30 a.m., heard from Josephstadt of the Crown Prince's approach ; he therefore ordered the 4th and 2nd Corps to evacuate the Swiep wood and to take up the partly entrenched line Chlum - Nedelist - Sendracic, as originally ordered. But General Mollinari (then command- ing the 4th Corps) objected, and moved slowly to Chlum. Count Thun (2nd Corps) also obeyed unwillingly. Benedek hesitated whether to send the 6th Corps to help the 4th and 2nd Corps ; he should have done so.

At 12 noon fifteen Prussian batteries at Racic and Habrina fired on the five Austrian batteries at Horenowes, and at 1 p.m. the I. Division Guards took Horenowes and drove the hostile batteries back. At 2.30 p.m. the VI. Corps, *viâ* Racic, occupied Sendracic, and drove the right of the 2nd Corps and the 2nd Light Cavalry Division on Lochenic. Thus this advance of the I. Division Guards and of the VI. Corps broke the flank march of the 2nd and 4th Corps—of the 2nd Corps the part that reached Nedelist was not effective — the 4th Corps got to Chlum and Rosberic, near which were eight batteries of the

Reserve Artillery, also the 3rd and 10th Corps. Behind them stood the Reserve (1st and 6th Corps, 2nd and 3rd Reserve Cavalry Divisions). Opposed to them in the north were the I. Division Guards, the VI. Corps on the line Maslowed-Sendracic - Trotina, with twelve batteries at Maslowed, and the VII. Division again in the Swiep wood.

Meantime on the Austrian left, at 8 a.m., the Elbe Army drove the Saxons out of Nechanitz, but as Herwarth repaired only the Nechanitz bridge and made no others, it was 11 a.m. before the XV. Division got across. He then moved the XV. Division and a cavalry brigade *viâ* Hradek against Ober Prim, and the XIV. Division *viâ* Lubno, against Problus. To stop this converging attack the Saxon Crown Prince counter-attacked *viâ* Hradek, at 12 noon, with his Saxons and part of the 8th Corps; this failed, and the XV. Division carried Prim, whilst the XIV. Division occupied Problus.

Then Benedek moved Edelsheim (1st Light Cavalry Division) from the left to the centre, instead of leaving him to look after the retreat through Pardubitz. The Elbe Army did no more.

In the north, at 1.30 p.m., the Crown Prince and the V. Corps entered Horenowes; at 2.45 p.m. the I. Division Guards took Chlum from the rear—a vital point, because it meant the junction of the I. and II. Armies. Then the Guards carried

AUSTRIAN POSITIONS AS ORDERED
July 3

Line 7½ miles
∴ 15 to the yard

Ô *Lipa* 3 C.

10 C.

○ *Tresowitz*

Saxons 8. C.

Popowitz
○

Sax. Cav.
I L.C.D.

N.

No VII.

Chlum o
▭ 4 C.

Nedelist
o
2 C.

2 L.C.D.

o
Sweti
I & 3 R.C.D.

o
Rosnitx
6 & I.C.

R.A.

Brixa o 2.R.C.D.

Stanford's Geog¹ Estab? London.

Rosberic, and at 3 p.m. the Crown Prince ordered the II. Division Guards to the same two places. Meantime the VI. Corps took Nedelist, and pushed the 2nd Corps behind the Elbe.

The 3rd Corps at Lipa and the 10th Corps and the 4th Corps began to retreat, but Benedek launched the 6th Corps to retake Chlum and Rosberic—the latter fell, but not the former, and the retreat of the 6th Corps was endangered by the advance of the VI. Corps on Sweti and on Lochenic bridge. Then Benedek sent the 1st Corps to retake Chlum; but as the Prussians were at Langenhof and at Sweti, the effort failed. The efforts to retake Chlum cost 10,000 men and 23 guns.

At 4.30 p.m. the Austrians retreated, the II. Cavalry Division worsting the 1st Reserve Cavalry Division and the 3rd Reserve Cavalry Division, near Langenhof. The retreat over the Elbe was gallantly covered by the Austrian guns and by the three other cavalry divisions. The Prussians bivouacked on the field, Moltke and the staff returning to Gitschin.

Remarks: The Prussian losses were 9,000; the Allies lost 44,000, including thousands of prisoners and 161 guns. The battle was between the Prussian infantry and the Austrian artillery. The I. Division Guards took Chlum easily, though the Austrians allege it was fiercely defended. Was it treacherously abandoned by Italian troops?

The woods lessened the deadliness of the needle gun. The Prussians did not use engineers enough; they were left on the lines of communication. They were in front in 1870–71 and in 1904–5.

Comments: (1) As to the Austrians, the fact is Benedek was interfered with, and he fought in order to settle the business—he would personally have preferred retreat. If there must be a battle, Benedek had better have stood over the Elbe, near Pardubitz. He fought with a river in his rear; but as he had twelve bridges and the guns of Königgrätz to help him, this was not an evil. Compare the case of Burnside at Fredericksburg, 1862, and of the Austrians at Solferino, 1859; contrast that of Benigsen at Friedland, 1807.

The position was angular, and that is always bad; the wings were in danger and the reserves should have been there. The bridges over the Bistritz should have been destroyed, because they were too far from the main position to be easily defended, and as the troops retired from them they were sure to suffer heavily. Hasty field entrenchments also, as in America, 1861–5, would have been of great service.

The left was a difficult problem. Glünicke suggests that the Saxon Crown Prince should have put the 8th Corps at Problus and the Saxons at Hradek, where that corps could cover the Pardubitz road. Perhaps a line from Nechanitz, along the Bistritz and the Lubno

ACTUAL POSITION OF AUSTRIANS
July 3

Line 9½ miles
∴ 13 to the yard

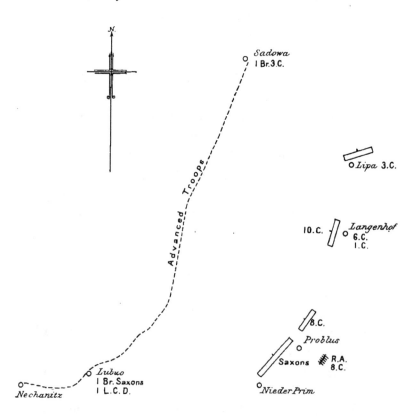

o *Horenowes*
2.C.

1 Br.
2 C. and 2 L.C.D.

o *Maslowed*
4.C.

B. Trotinke

Chlum
o ½ A.RA.
1 R.C.D.

Elbe R.

o
Sweti 3.R.C.D.

o *Rosnitz*
½ A.R.A.

o *Briza*
2 . R.C.D

heights, would have been preferable. The Saxon Crown Prince unwisely used up his men in a counter-attack. The centre was well occupied.

The right was the crucial point; the works there were useless. The 4th Corps was right in occupying Maslowed, but it should have faced north, and so should the 2nd Corps, and both corps should not have paid so much attention to the Swiep wood. They should have held Horenowes, with their right on the Trotina R., the bridge over which should have been destroyed, and part of the reserve should have supported them. Festetic (4th Corps) should have told the Chief of Staff that he had occupied Maslowed. Fact is, he was severely wounded, and thus, instead of sealing up the VII. Division in the wood by gun-fire, the 4th Corps acted against the wood, in spite of Benedek's distinct order. Worse still, Count Thun employed his 2nd Corps for the same purpose.

All these evils arose from the fact that Benedek did not scout with cavalry to the north, and did not pay sufficient regard to the telegram from Josephstadt at 11.30 a.m. The cavalry could have delayed the Crown Prince; the 4th and 2nd Corps could then have annihilated the VII. Division, and the 10th and 3rd Corps routed the I. Army. The II. Army would have been helpless. No doubt Mollinari (4th Corps) and Thun thought that in Fransecky (VII. Division) they had found the extreme right of the Prussians. Probably Benedek's spies led him to think that the Crown Prince was moving in the same line as Frederick Charles, so as to threaten the Pardubitz route to Vienna. This would explain why he did not in the morning crush the I. Army Divisions across the Bistritz; he thought them stronger than they were. Besides, he argued that even if the II. Army were coming on his right, the bad roads and anxiety for its line of communications would check it till he had defeated the I. Army.

He stated only one line of retreat instead of naming a line of retreat for each corps. The redeeming feature was the magnificent fighting of the Austrian cavalry and artillery in covering the retreat.

(2) As to the Prussians, the Elbe Army stopped after taking Problus, and did not threaten the Pardubitz route because the XVI. Division was delayed at Nechanitz by allowing the Cavalry Division Alvensleben to go over first. Frederick Charles's men fought splendidly, but the Prince should have stopped west of the Bistritz and waited there for the enveloping movements of the two wings, but he had to push on because he had foolishly sent the VII. Division to Cerekwitz over the river; hence his losses. True it is that the error about Fransecky turned out well, because it induced the 4th and 2nd Corps to turn their attention to the wrong quarter. The late arrival

5

of the Crown Prince was due to the retention of the mass of his army on the east bank of the Elbe during July 2, and to Bonin's (I. Corps) slowness.

The Prussian cavalry was not wisely employed ; it was much split up ; it would have been better to place the Cavalry Corps on the right of the Elbe Army, and the Cavalry Division on the left of the Crown Prince.

The pursuit, too, was weak, nor did the cavalry follow the enemy closely, but even a victorious army is disorganised after a great battle. At Königgrätz it is to be noticed that the Prussians passed from the defensive to the offensive ; compare the Allies at Waterloo.

CHAPTER X

OPERATIONS TO THE CLOSE OF THE WAR,
JULY 4–22

ON July 4 Benedek retired in three columns, making for Zwittau, and decided to move his mass to Olmütz, detaching, however, the 10th Corps and all the cavalry (except the 2nd Light Cavalry Division) to proceed by rail and road to Vienna. The main body reached Olmütz on the 11th.

On July 4 the Prussians rested, their communications being in an unsatisfactory condition. On July 5 the Cavalry Division Hartmann crossed at Pardubitz, the II. Army (except VI. Corps left to watch Königgrätz and Josephstadt) moved on Pardubitz, the I. Army on Prelauc, Elbe Army along the Elbe west of Prelauc. The last Army despatched the Guard Landwehr to Prague, which it occupied July 8 : this opened the railway Turnau-Prague-Pardubitz, but no traffic could pass till the 13th. The two Elbe fortresses and Theresienstadt blocked the other railways.

On July 6 the Prussians discovered the enemy's retreat on Olmütz. Moltke therefore moved II

Army on Olmütz (if attacked by Benedek, it was to retire on Silesia and the I. Army would return and "nutcracker" the Austrians; it would also establish a new line of communications *viá* Glatz, abandoning the Königinhof line upon which the VI. Corps could rejoin the Crown Prince—this new line was not used), I. Army on Brünn, Elbe Army on Znaim.

On July 11 the new Austrian Commander-in-Chief, the Archduke Albert, directed Benedek to entrain to Vienna all his corps except the 6th Corps. Consequently he at once entrained the 3rd Corps, which reached Vienna next day; on the 13th the Saxons entrained, of whom part thus reached the capital, part did not; on the 14th 2nd and 4th Corps marched on the west bank of the March R. (they took this route because it was the better road and they were ignorant of II. Army's approach, but it was an error); on the 15th the 8th Corps followed, and by the east bank the 1st Corps, part of the Saxons, and the Reserve Artillery; the 6th Corps moved down the Waag R., the Archduke having ordered that only a small garrison should stop at Olmütz.

When the Archduke and General von John reached Vienna on July 13, they found 92,000 men and 364 guns at Olmütz, 41,000 and 106 guns on the way to Vienna, 9,000 cavalry and 72 guns on the R. Thaya, 3rd Corps and 10th Corps at Vienna, except brigade Mondel left at

Lundenburg; besides 57,000 men and 120 guns coming from Italy. Total, 216,000 and 718 guns. The real hope, however, was in the intervention of Napoléon III., who should have actively joined Austria, and Moltke found Bismarck's influence paralysing. The capital itself was covered by works at Florisdorf.

On July 12 and 13 the I. Army entered Brünn, and Elbe Army Znaim. The II. Army reached Prossnitz, the cavalry striking the 2nd Corps, and the Crown Prince concluded he had struck Benedek's rear. He therefore directed the Guards and VI. Corps on Brünn, leaving only I. Corps and V. Corps at Prossnitz. This was an error; he should with all his forces have struck at Benedek.

ACTION OF TOBITSCHAU, July 15

The 2nd and 4th Corps were passing down the right bank of the R. March, followed by the 8th Corps, which at Tobitschau was assailed by I. Corps and part of the Cavalry Division Hartmann. Here Bredow's V. Cuirassiers charged four batteries and captured 18 guns. The Archduke Leopold retired his corps over the March to Prerau. The Prussian cavalry also, though without success, attacked the 1st Corps at Prerau. *Tobitschau, July 15. Plan No. IX.*

The I. Army was then twisted eastwards on Lundenburg and damaged the rail, July 15,

and the Elbe Army also twisted east *via* Laa—
this was to assist the Crown Prince. Upon this
the brigade Mondel left for Blumenau, and
Benedek fetched the 4th and 2nd Corps over to
the east bank of the March R., and moved them
down together with the 1st, 8th, and 6th Corps,
through the Little Carpathians.

On July 16 the Crown Prince's troops foolishly
broke a railway bridge at Prerau, thus cutting
connection with Upper Silesia. On July 17
the Guards and VI. Corps reached Brünn, and
Moltke ordered a march on to the Danube,
I. Army along the March R., II. Army *via*
Nikolsburg. The question of bombarding the
Vienna works led to differences between Moltke
and Bismarck—the former said the guns must
come from Dresden, the latter said there was
no time for this, as France might interfere. The
fact was that Bismarck did not want the Prussians
to enter Vienna in triumph, because it would
permanently alienate Austria. The King decided
in favour of the statesman; compare the similar
dispute before Paris, 1870–71.

On July 18 the Elbe Army moved on Ganners-
dorf, part of the I. Army down the west bank
of the March, and down the east bank the VIII.
and V. Divisions. In the rear, west of the river,
marched the Guards, the VI. Corps and the V.
Corps, the I. Corps investing Olmütz. On July 19
Moltke, ignorant how many Austrians were at

Vienna, ordered a concentration behind the
Russbach and the I. Army to surprise Pressburg—
a vital point, because if it fell Benedek's route
to Vienna must be *viá* Komorn. On July 20
one brigade of the 2nd Corps (which corps did 150
miles in 8 days) went to support brigade Mondel
of 10th Corps at Blumenau. Next day Mondel
was further reinforced up to 27 battalions,
besides cavalry and guns. At Stampfen Fransecky (VII. Division) had the VII. and VIII.
Divisions and Cavalry Division Hann, *i.e.* 16,000
men.

COMBAT AT BLUMENAU, JULY 22

Fransecky's plan was to contain in front and Blumenau,
to turn the enemy's right *viá* Marienthal. At July 22.
7.30 a.m. he was told the armistice would begin Plan
No. X.
at noon. He slowly moved against Mondel's Plan
XIV.
front, whilst the turning force arrived on the in Glünicke.
Gemsenberg. At noon hostilities ceased.

Comments : (1) Fransecky thought he had only
a brigade to deal with ; his tactics were excellent ;
(2) Austrian guns did well.

The Prussians occupied the following positions :
Elbe Army, I. and II. Armies between Brünn
and Vienna, Mülbe's Landwehr at Brünn, half
the I. Corps and Knoblesdorf before Olmütz,
Stolberg in Silesia, Guard Landwehr at Prague,
Landwehr in Saxony and the garrison towns.

France had intervened and procured the

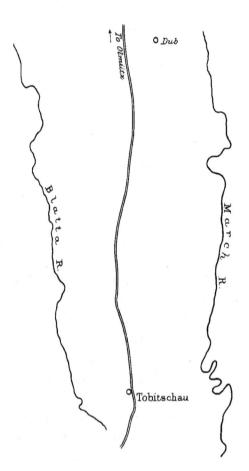

To Olmütz

○ *Dub*

Blatta R.

March R.

○ Tobitschau

Tr

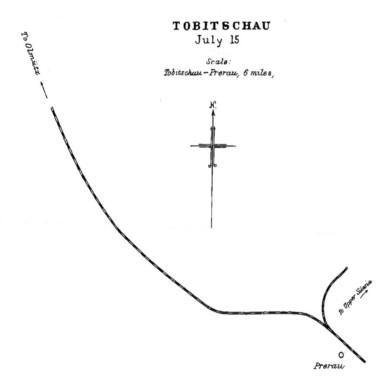

TOBITSCHAU
July 15

Scale:
Tobitschau – Prerau, 6 miles,

N.

To Olmütz

To Upper Silesia

Prerau

Zubeck

armistice (July 22) of Nikolsburg, which in August became the Treaty of Prague—(1) Austria excluded from Germany; (2) North Germany to be under Prussia; (3) Schleswig-Holstein, Hanover, electorate of Hesse-Kassel, Duchy of Nassau, Frankfurt to Prussia; (4) Venetia to Italy; (5) Austria to pay £3,000,000. The troops returned suffering from cholera.

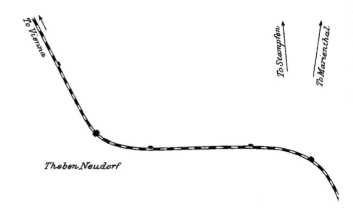

Theben Neudorf

BLUMENAU
.July 22

Theatre, very mountainous

Scale :
Blumenau – Pressburg 3½ miles

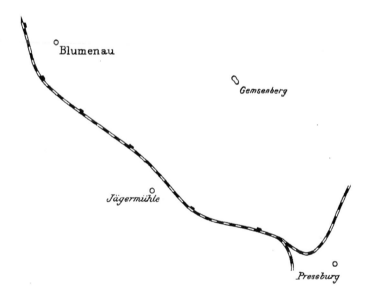

CHAPTER XI

TACTICAL REMARKS AND STRATEGIC COMMENTS

INFANTRY: the Austrian tactics were bad. They believed in the offensive with the bayonet.; they used battalion-columns of double companies with very few skirmishers and hardly any fire-preparation; hence heavy losses, as at Trautenau and Chlum. The weapon was the Lorenz rifled muzzle-loader (longer ranged than the needle-gun), but the men were poor shots.

The Prussians used company-columns with numerous skirmishers; the weapon was the needle-gun (range of 300 yards), whose advantages were the facts that it could be loaded quickly and when the soldier was lying down. The general effect of breech-loaders was to cause company-columns to supersede battalion-columns, because the latter could not so easily dissolve into skirmishing lines. In the Prussian infantry initiative was highly developed.

Cavalry: They never broke formed infantry. There were great cavalry combats on July 3, in which the Austrians came off best; and note the splendid work of Bredow at Tobitschau.

Artillery: Many Prussian guns were smooth-bores, all the Austrian rifled; the Prussians did not mass their guns, the Austrians did. Both sides had reserve artillery, which is unwise. The Austrian guns were 2·7 per 1,000 infantry, the Prussian 3·6. The Prussian range was 1,500 yards, but the guns were not pushed to the front; the Austrian guns were well handled. Breech-loading guns were adopted after this war.

STRATEGIC COMMENTS

(1) *Strategic Work of the Cavalry.*—After Königgrätz the Prussians lost touch of the enemy, because they did not send their cavalry ahead. In fact, all through the campaign all the Armies used their horsemen badly; the I. and II. Armies kept their cavalry in rear, and their spies, who were good, gave more information than was gained by their mounted arm. The only good strategic work done by the cavalry was done by Hartmann after July 3. Frederick Charles, by keeping back his Cavalry Corps, was ignorant of the real strength of the Saxon Crown Prince at München-grätz. Otherwise he could have contained that Prince and Clam Gallas, and with the rest of his force reached Gitschin; in other words, he gave Benedek a chance on June 28 of crushing

the Crown Prince. On July 1 and 2 the Prussian cavalry did not ascertain the Austrian positions. Neither side raided the enemy's communications, perhaps because their horsemen had no rifles; but the whole question of the utility of cavalry raids is much debated.

(2) *Benedek and the Austrian Plan of Campaign.*—The plan reminds one of eighteenth-century war; the best thing would have been to resign Venetia, keep only a small force there to hold back the Italians, place another containing army at Olmütz and enter Saxony with their main body, joining there the Saxons and possibly the Bavarians. Want of money delayed their mobilisation, and Benedek found himself thrown on the defensive, though personally he had decided on an offensive campaign. We call this offensive his first plan, which became impossible owing to the tardy mobilisation. His second plan was merely to mass near Josephstadt; his third to move in mass against the I. Army whilst holding the II. Army. This plan he discarded on June 28, at 8 p.m., and formed his fourth plan, viz. fight in the Dubenetz position. On the 30th he arranged a fifth plan, viz. to retreat; and on July 2 his sixth and final plan—fight at Königgrätz.

Benedek had the interior position, and if he had acted on Napoleonic principles should have been victorious. His correct plan should have been to reinforce the Saxon Prince with one more corps and to give him clear instructions to contain the Elbe and I. Armies, not on the Iser R. but right up north in the mountain passes. This would have allowed of sufficient elbow-room for interior line action. He could then have turned his mass against the Crown Prince, who should have been his objective, because he was nearer and more threatening to the Austrian communications (compare the Archduke Charles's error, when in 1809 he failed to crush the French centre at Abensberg and turned off against the more distant French left at Ratisbon). Benedek held neither army, and thus lost the strategic advantage of his interior position and exposed himself to its tactical disadvantages, *i.e.* the fire action of converging masses. In fact, Benedek could not manage interior lines, nor did he ever understand the Crown Prince's march.

As to details, the Austrian commander left Gablenz in the lurch though the latter pointed out his danger; his orders to the Saxon Crown Prince were very conflicting, *e.g.* the two orders on the 26th, and on the 27th, in reply to the Saxon Prince's, "What am I to do?" Benedek telegraphed, "I shall be in Miletin on June 29."

All during June 26, 27, and 28 he had a chance of holding the I. Army and of crushing the II. Army; *e.g.* on the 26th the Crown Prince's forces were in three separated columns, and on the 27th Frederick Charles had spared the Saxons and the 1st Corps, and Bonin had retired.

His retreat on Olmütz was on the whole judicious, because Vienna was too far away, and there were no good defensible positions on the route. Olmütz would to a safe refuge; but how dangerous that may be is shown by the fate of Bazaine, 1870. The limited eccentric retreat to Olmütz was no doubt intended to act as a flank defence of Vienna and to force the victors to separate; at the same time such a flank retreat is not of much avail, unless the army executing it is capable of the offensive. The one argument in favour of a retreat on Vienna was that the victorious troops from Italy would be found there. The Archduke Albert was no doubt right later on in calling Benedek to Vienna.

Throughout his book on 1866 Colonel Glünicke is too hard on Benedek, who was a really able tactician, as he had proved at Solferino, and who was much hampered by interference from high quarters. It is true, however, that he had little strategic knowledge. "Your Majesty, I am no strategist," he told his Sovereign.

(3) *Moltke and the Prussian Plan.*—The wisdom or unwisdom of Moltke's plan is the great crux of this campaign. It is best to consider first the two great opposing principles of strategy—Interior Lines *v.* Exterior Lines.

Napoléon is the chief exponent of the former,

Moltke of the latter; the disadvantages of the single or interior line are that the army acting on it may be crushed between two allied armies acting from divergent bases or rather zones of strategic deployment—note the cases of Napoléon crushed at Waterloo, 1815, between Wellington and Blücher, and crushed at Leipzig, 1813, between the converging armies of the Allies— and that the crowded advance increases the losses. Its great advantage is that the troops are well in hand. The disadvantage of double or exterior lines is that the armies acting on them may be held apart and beaten in detail—note the Austrians and Sardinians beaten thus by Napoléon, 1796, and the Austrians alone similarly routed by the same conqueror round Mantua, 1796–7, and Frémont and Shields worsted in the same manner by Stonewall Jackson, 1862. Their great advantages are that they necessarily give greater play to modern fire-arms, that they produce more striking results, and that supply is facilitated.

Neither form can be said to be superior to the other; it depends upon circumstances. Given no railways, no telegraphs, and no very large armies, the interior line is to be preferred; and, indeed, under such conditions, it had been generally successful up to 1813. But the interior line requires great mobility, and in the commander surpassing genius; and in 1813, 1814, 1815, even the French monarch had been worsted by exterior line forces, as had Lee at the close of the Secession War, 1865.

One of the distinctions between the two systems is that on the interior line the tendency is to concentrate before the battle, whereas on exterior lines the tendency is to concentrate during the battle. Napoléon and Ney concentrated at Quatre Bras, and then approached Waterloo; the Allied Armies united on that field. The I. and II. Armies, in 1866, concentrated at Königgrätz. Those armies, indeed, wanted to unite before the battle, but Molte declined to permit this. If Napoléon had conducted the Prussian campaign he would probably have massed in S.W. Silesia, and moved straight on Vienna; but not only were the railways not capable of such a task, but also the King was opposed (and rightly) to such drastic action. Exceptions no doubt there are, as when Napoléon concentrated Ney with himself on the field of Bautzen, 1813. It should be added that a re-entrant base, or rather zone of strategic deployment, favours the exterior lines.

Now, to apply these principles to 1866. The Prussian Armies detrained thus: Elbe Army at Halle, I. Army near Kottbus, II. Army near Neisse, I. Corps as connecting link at Görlitz—this meant an arc of 276 miles. By the orders of May 30 Elbe Army moved to Torgau, I. Army on Görlitz, II. Army to Landshut with I. Corps added to it—this meant an arc of 156 miles.

By the orders of June 12 the Elbe Army stopped at Torgau, I. Army held the front, Görlitz-Landshut, II. Army returned towards Neisse—this meant an arc of 208 miles. By the orders of June 22 Gitschin was given as the point of concentration.

Those who regard Moltke's strategic concentration as judicious argue thus: Berlin and Silesia had to be protected, and this necessitated the at first dangerous separation of the armies; but Moltke then decided to unite all his forces by moving them into Bohemia—in fact, to work on double or exterior lines. He relied on Benedek being unable to act on interior line with the ability of a Napoléon. His plan was to "nutcracker" Benedek. Politics had stayed his hand till June 14, the date of the hostile vote of the Federal Diet. His original idea was to have two corps in Silesia, the Elbe Army to hold the Saxons, and his main army at Görlitz. He first linked the I. and II. Armies by means of the I. Corps; he then transferred that corps to the II. Army, and, not knowing if the Austrians would move into Silesia or into Saxony, wisely decided on the offensive (June 16), and as the Crown Prince might be assailed, gave him the Guards. He calculated that the Elbe Army and I. Army could reach the Iser R. before Benedek could, and he argued that even alone they could, with the needle-gun, hold their own till the

II. Army should arrive. In other words, he took into account not only strategy, but also tactics. To secure a favourable result he saw that he must select the correct point of concentration (Gitschin), and also start the armies at the correct time. The plan turned out well; and when Moltke found that Gitschin was not to be the battlefield, he simply still kept the armies separate and carried out his idea at Königgrätz in accord with his saying, "March divided, fight concentrated." The strengthening of the II. Army, by adding to it the I. Corps and the Guards, has been justified on the ground of the difficult passes it had to traverse, of the importance of its work, and of the menace to Silesia involved in Benedek's position.

On the other hand, many criticisms have been levelled at Moltke's general idea, and there is no doubt that his strategic concentration in 1870 was utterly different from that in 1866, that the latter was at first dangerous, and that his selection of Gitschin was mistaken. Moltke, defending his lengthy arc of 276 miles, at times puts it down to uncertainty whether Benedek would aim at Berlin or at Breslau, at times puts it down to the position of Saxony.

Moltke's orders of May 30, reducing the arc to 156 miles, clearly show that he saw the danger of his original concentration; and besides, he vacillated about the I. Corps—at first it was to

6

be a connecting link, then it was added to the II. Army.

From June 10 the strategic front was linear or cordon-like, a thing which Napoléon abominated; and this was because the Prussians had not previously prepared supplies in the zone of assembly —Napoléon always did this.

Map II. in Bonnal. General F. C. Bonnal, in his well-known work on Sadowa, suggests that Moltke should have massed the Elbe Army at Torgau to cover Berlin, and the I. and II. Armies east of Gorlitz as the mass of manœuvre, with the V. and VI. Corps south of Breslau to protect Silesia. Thus would Berlin and Breslau be protected, the Elbe Army and the two corps being containing forces; but Moltke did not understand the value of such a force, nor did he in 1870; *e.g.* he never seemed to think that the V. and VI. Corps could contain Benedek, and therefore he unwisely gave the Crown Prince two more corps, and thus converted what should have been a covering force into the main army; and again, he was so fearful of the Elbe Army being left face to face with the Saxons that he reinforced it with Mülbe's troops.

The move to Neisse under the orders of June 12 caused a second dangerous separation on an arc of 208 miles.

(4) *Frederick Charles.*—his slowness—six miles a day—nearly ruined the whole of Moltke's combination. The latter urged him on during the

28th, twice during the 29th, and also during the 30th. His slowness was due to the heat, to what he considered the dangerous weakness of his army, to the rearward position of his cavalry, which, therefore, could not tell him he had only two corps to oppose (not three as he supposed), to waiting for the Elbe Army, and, more than all, to the divisional arrangement which he adopted. This last necessitated a separate road for each division—not for each corps as in 1870—and also the despatch of orders to twelve distinct heads, viz. ten divisional commanders, one cavalry commander, and the artillery reserve. As a fact, he put the Crown Prince in some danger.

At Münchengrätz he held, and rightly, that the Austrians believed in the doctrine of positions; he therefore concluded they would stand fast; hence his enveloping movement. What he should have done was to contain the Saxon Prince and to hurry the rest of his forces on Gitschin *viâ* Turnau, and thus sever the Saxon Prince from Benedek. His artillery reserve too was excessive, 96 out of 300 guns.

(5) *Bonin and Clam Gallas.*—General Bonin (I. Corps) acted badly on June 27 and on July 3; Clam Gallas was incompetent and insubordinate. He abandoned Turnau in spite of orders, and thus gave up the shorter route to Gitschin and endangered his union with the main army. It would seem that he was thinking of Prague rather than

of Gitschin. It must be admitted that he never had clear instructions from his chief.

(6) *The Railways and Prussian Supply.*—The supply system was territorial and depended on railways. Requisitions were paid for by cheques. On the Iser R. and in marching to the Bistritz the I. Army suffered from lack of food. The railways were not good; up to July 8 there was no line available beyond Turnau, and after that date only one. The Prerau line to Silesia was rendered useless by the Prussians destroying the Prerau bridge. On July 19 the line Turnau-Prague-Pardubitz-Lundenburg was open, but only six trains could come per day. Königgrätz and Josephstadt and Königstein were not besieged because their fall would not open another railway. The food for the Prussians was procured by requisition from the magazines or by quartering the troops on the people. The Prussians did not follow up the field armies quickly enough with Landwehr, who should guard the railways and invest and garrison the fortresses; they would thus have saved many field troops. The fact is that the King did not believe in Landwehr.

(7) *Detachments.*—The test of the wisdom of a detachment is, does it or does it not assist the main action? The action of the VI. Corps in feinting on the Silesian frontier had considerable effect on the Austrians; and likewise the detached forces in Southern Silesia. Compare the effect

on the French produced by a German force in
Baden, 1870. One of the most foolish of detachments was the despatch of Montbrun's Cavalry,
1811–12, to Alicante in Spain, by which Mar-
mont was deprived of valuable information.

(8) *Initiative, Value of.*—If the Prussians had
moved early in June they would have gained
much, and again if they had moved on June 21;
but they could not, because by orders of June 12
the II. Army had gone to Neisse and had to
countermarch. An earlier move would also have
benefited the Austrians, but want of money pre-
vented this.

(9) *Politics.*—Whether politics should affect
military operations is a constant subject of debate.
It is admitted that statesmen must decide the
outbreak and the conclusion of a war, and Clause-
witz, the greatest of strategic authorities, argues
that they should control the operations as they
proceed, though his opinion is not shared by all
other authorities. Politics affected this war at
the outset, for the King rightly held that if he
acted hurriedly he would risk his chances of
becoming German Emperor; politics dictated the
move of the II. Army to the Neisse position,
under the orders of June 12; politics paralysed
the Prussian action, not only just before Königgrätz, but all during the pursuit; politics, in the
person of Bismarck, overruled Moltke at the
very close of the campaign; and, in my opinion,

in every instance the Iron Chancellor was right—
he gauged the situation (compare the dispute
before Paris, 1870–71). In fact, the whole question of policy affecting military operations resolves
itself into a question as to whether the policy is
sound or not, and I admit that the move to
Neisse (by the orders of June 12), caused by the
Crown Prince's anxiety for Silesia, was a case of
unwise policy.

(10) *Position of Headquarters.*—The presence
of the monarch in the field, unless he is a genius,
is a nuisance. The King was attended by Bismarck, without whom he could not have dealt
with political issues, and that statesman fre-
quently differed from Moltke. This may or may
not have been an evil, but, in any case, if the
King did appear he should have arrived earlier
than he did, and should not have stopped at
Gitschin on July 2, thus losing many hours for
the despatch of orders. If Moltke had appeared
earlier, Frederick Charles would have been more
rapid, and the Crown Prince would not have
detached the VI. Corps to Habelschwerdt.
Napoléon always took the field at the outset of
a campaign, and was attended by no politicians;
but the French Sovereign was a consummate
genius.

LIST OF QUESTIONS

1. State cause of the war, and the combatants on either side.

2. Describe the Austrian and Prussian military systems.

3. State the strength of the various armies.

4. Describe the theatre of operations.

5. Sketch the military operations up to June 22 (1) dealing with the Saxons and Austrians, (2) dealing with the Prussians. Note the dates May 12, May 30, June 12, and June 22.

6. What advantages were gained by invading Saxony?

7. Describe briefly the operations of the Elbe Army and of the I. Army, June 23-29.

8. With rough plan describe the Battle of Gitschin, adding tactical comments.

9. Consider if Benedek could have crushed the Crown Prince on June 26, 27, and 28, and how he could have done so.

10. What errors marred the Crown Prince's march through the mountains?

11. With rough plan describe the Trautenau action, and comment on it.

12. With rough plan describe the Skalitz action, and comment on it.

13. Assuming that Benedek, instead of fighting at Königgrätz, had crossed and stood behind the Elbe, how could Moltke have dealt with him?

14. Draw rough plan of the Battle of Königgrätz and place the Austrian troops (1) as ordered, (2) as actually posted.

15. Describe the events of the great battle.

16. Criticise Benedek's tactics in the battle.

17. What errors do you consider the Prussians committed in the battle?

18. Describe generally the operations from July 4 to the end of the war.

19. Comment on the tactics of the three arms on both sides.

20. Consider the strategic work of the Cavalry.

21. Criticise Benedek's plans of campaign. Suggest an alternative.

22. Examine the wisdom or unwisdom of Moltke's leading. Suggest an alternative course of action.

23. Criticise Frederick Charles's action.

24. Comment on the railway work, on detachments, on the value of initiative.

25. Show how politics affected this campaign.